# GRANDPA'S STORIES

## Volume 10

### Tales of the Wild West Series

## Rick Steber

### Illustrations by Don Gray

NOTE
*GRANDPA'S STORIES* is the tenth book in the
Tales of the Wild West Series


*GRANDPA'S STORIES*
Volume 10
Tales of the Wild West Series

**Bonanza Publishing**
Box 204
Prineville, Oregon 97754

# Tales of the Wild West

# INTRODUCTION

Great-Grandpa came west in a covered wagon. He grew up riding a horse to and from school. He helped farm with horses and when the family traveled it was by horse and buggy. In his long life he lived to see the advent of the automobile, machinery replace horses on the farm, and aviation progress from a few barnstorming pilots hop-scotching across the country to jet aircraft thundering across the sky, and finally man walking on the moon.

When he was seated in his favorite rocking chair, children scattered at his feet, Great-Grandpa's eyes sparkled as lively as they must have in his youth. He told stories that exuberantly recounted the past and his words painted vivid pictures of his life on the western frontier as a pioneer, miner, freighter, stage driver, trapper, logger, homesteader or buckaroo.

At the end of each story he sat in silence and patiently waited for one of the children to implore, "Tell us another story, please."

Then he grinned, leaned back and began, "This story happened a long, looong, looooog time ago...."

# THE WILDCAT

"Grandpa, tell us a story, the one about the wildcat that almost got you," requested one of the grandkids.

Grandpa lit his pipe, blew out a cloud of smoke and drawled, "I don't rightly remember which wildcat story that might've been."

"The one in the mine!" several of the children cried in unison. Grandpa smiled and set the pipe aside.

"Sure you wanna hear that one again?"

"Yeah! Yeah!"

"Okay. This here story happened on the twenty-first day of January, nineteen ought six. I was working as a mucker in the Inkerman Mine. Anybody know what a mucker does? A mucker works down in the ground, shoveling ore into the mine cars.

"Anyway, that day my crew was working at the 325-foot level. We were taking our lunch break, sitting in a circle, when all of a sudden this here wildcat landed right in the middle of us. Lands on its feet, stays crouched down, acts dazed.

"Turned out, later when we put it all together, this cat must have fallen down the shaft and hit a cross bar which flipped it into the opening where we were.

"The cat came to its senses, showed its teeth, hissed and snarled real nasty-like, low and menacing. Like this, 'RRRARR.'

"I've never seen men move so fast. We jumped up, grabbed picks and drills and swung them to keep the cat at bay. A lucky blow finally ended the battle.

"After that we came topside and spent the remainder of the day showing off our prize and toasting our courage."

# MY TRIP WEST

"I knew I never wanted to spend another winter in Montana, so the fall of 1875 I headed for the west coast," Eli Glover said. "I rode my horse over the Rockies and upon reaching the Columbia River I sold my horse and took passage on one of the many ships plying the river.

"My voyage went without incident until we reached the John Day Rapids. I was on deck, standing on the bow as we threaded our way through the white water and exposed boulders. All of a sudden there was a muffled roar, like a piece of flannel being ripped, and I was thrown against the railing. A man near me got to his feet and wanted to know if we were going to sink. I looked over the side, saw a gaping hole in the hull and told him, 'Without a doubt.'

"The captain steered for shore but the engine room filled with water and drowned the engines. Our momentum carried us forward but when it became evident we were not going to run aground two crewmen jumped into the swirling water and were able to secure a safety line to a boulder on shore. The line came taut, the ship swung around and we were left only a scant twenty feet out in the current.

"We counted our blessings as a small lifeboat was put over the side and ferried passengers to shore. We built a huge driftwood bonfire and food was brought from the ship. All the liquor on board was considered fair plunder.

"We kept the fire burning and generally made a party of our unfortunate predicament. Had anyone attempted to liberate us, we might have resisted. But by the following afternoon, with food and drink running low, we were very appreciative when the steamer *Owyhee* came to our rescue."

# JUST FOR LUCK

"When you hear this story you might think I'm pulling your leg, but I'll prove it's true," M.L. Peterson claimed.

"Back in the summer of 1878 the Bannock Indians went on the warpath. One evening at dusk a raiding party attacked me. In the exchange of gunfire I took a slug in my hip. I held the off the Indians until darkness settled in and then managed to slip away.

"Although my wound did not bleed much it gave me a great deal of discomfort. I had no choice but to keep on the move, trying to put distance between myself and the Indians. In the long run that proved beneficial because my constant movement prevented me from stiffening up.

"After traveling three days and nights, existing only on leaves and water, my strength was beginning to fail and I was ready to lie down and meet my maker. But, as luck would have it, I stumbled upon a camp of soldiers.

"The company doctor removed the bullet imbedded in my hip. However, in the days that followed, the pain did not go away. At last, having given the matter considerable thought, I told the doctor, 'I was shot at close range and by all rights the bullet should have gone clean through me. I believe the slug struck one of the metal buttons on my overalls and drove it into me.'

"I even showed him where a button was missing. He gave me an examination and said no, that there were no foreign objects lodged in my body. Well, I knew he was wrong but what could I do?

"I learned to live with the constant pain. After years of suffering I went to another doctor. He operated and found this. It's kind of dinged but you can clearly see it is a metal button. Ever since then, just for luck, I've carried this button in my pocket."

# PIE JOHN

"I'll admit, the name 'Pie John' is an unusual handle to have someone hang on you," grinned Pie John Wintjen. "It came about this way....

"Was the winter of '52. I was in partners on the Table Rock Billiard Saloon in Jacksonville, Oregon. Gold had been struck and ten thousand men crowded in and were living in shacks and in tents.

"One day I made a few loaves of bread and discovered that a hungry miner would pay handsomely for a slice of home-cooked bread. That same day my partner and I added a bakery onto the saloon. Business was so good we soon ran out of flour. There was no flour to be had anywhere in town.

"It was brought to my attention that one Peter Britt, a local photographer, was hoarding a fifty-pound sack of flour. I paid him a visit, offered him a fantastic price for his flour but he refused to sell. I informed him he was acting in a very selfish and unsociable manner, especially considering it was the Christmas season.

"After that, when the miners came to me wanting baked goods I told them that Mr. Britt had the only flour in town and that he refused to sell it. The men were a very discontented lot and word soon reached Mr. Britt that, for his own safety and welfare, he should name a price and sell his sack of flour.

"To make a long story short, Mr. Britt informed me he was willing to sell but he wanted a dollar a pound for his flour. I bought it all and set about making apple pies. I sold pie by the piece and made a substantial profit, as well as earning my nickname of 'Pie John'."

# GRANDFATHER AND THE WOLVES

Grandfather Soman was a logger. He lived with his family in a cabin tucked way back in the woods.

One cold winter the Somans were running low on supplies. Grandfather gathered his sons around him and told them, "I'll snowshoe into the settlement. You stay here and look out after your mother."

That evening as the family ate supper they listened, expecting the familiar "halloo" from up the trail. But there was no sound. They waited a few more hours and finally Grandmother said, "Boys, something must have happened to your father. You better go look for him."

The boys pulled on their coats and fur hats. They took their rifles down from the pegs on the wall and stepped out into the night. The sky had cleared and a cold white moon was out. Stars were splashed across the heavens and the Northern Lights swept back and forth in colored bars. As the boys followed along the trail the snow, crunching under their weight, was the only sound, until one of the boys raised his hand and said, "Hold up. I hear something. Wolves!

The pack was running something, probably a deer, and then the chorus changed. The wolves became more excited, like they do when the kill is close at hand. The boys hurried forward and at last broke into a small clearing where they saw the pack of wolves running in circles, pawing at the snow, trying to dig under a wooden water trough tipped upside down. The boys fired into the air, the wolves ran away and slowly the water trough moved and mysteriously rolled over. The dark outline of a man became visible and a voice boomed out, "Halloo. Boys, it's me. You found me just in the nick of time."

# HONESTY PAYS

Old man Phillips kicked around from here to there and when he needed money he worked odd jobs. According to Phillips, "There came the day I had the chance to prove I was something more than just a common, ordinary bum.

"That day I happened to spy a small chamois bag lying in the gutter. I picked it up, loosened the drawstring and poured two diamond rings into my hand. For the longest time I stood staring at them.

"I knew someone would be looking for the rings so I read the Lost and Found column in the newspaper. Sure enough, there was an advertisement by a woman named Mrs. Carty. It gave her address. I went there, asked her to describe the rings. She did and I handed her the bag. She gave me a reward, not a big reward but a nice reward. I was happy.

"Then a newspaper man looked me up, interviewed me and took my picture. The story ran in the afternoon edition. By nightfall my friends were teasing me, saying I was an idiot for returning the rings. And they had the nerve to hit me up, wanting me to loan them money from my reward. I gave away everything I had except for a few dollars. This I used to celebrate. But my celebration was cut short when police arrested me for singing *Oh, Susanna* on a street corner and tossed me in jail.

"What I learned from all of this is that it's a fine and decent thing for a man to be honest but sometimes it doesn't pay him to advertise the fact. Then again, in the long run everything did work out. Police chief Jenkins ordered me released, gave me a handshake and a dollar bill, and told me, 'Phillips, you're an honest ol' bum,' and that meant more to me than anything."

# THE OLD CABIN

"Back in the year eighteen and sixty-four, I was prospecting with three partners," Bill Kelly related. "We planned to throw together a log cabin before winter set in but kept putting it off since we were finding gold enough to hold promise but not enough to make us rich.

"Then along came the first big storm. We thought we could ride it out but our tent leaked like a sieve and the ditch we dug to protect us washed out. We were plumb uncomfortable. And to make matters worse the flour and coffee got soggy, the jerky molded and there was not a stick of dry firewood wood to be found.

"For thirty straight days it rained and then the weather cleared and we straight to work building a cabin and stockpiling wood. The first snow came, drifted against the cabin and we were warm and snug. The thing I most remember were the wolves serenading us and those times I would awaken from a dead sleep and hear the wolves scratching at the logs by my head and feel their hot breath between breaks in the chinking. It makes my skin crawl even now.

"It got to where our provisions were running mighty low. We were fearful we might starve to death but then the warm weather hit, the sun popped out and began melting the snow and, here and there, green grass began to poke through the snow. That was a beautiful sight.

"We worked our claim until the color played out. Then we hoisted up our packs and went our separate ways. As far as I know, our cabin was never used again, and by now she's probably caved in on herself."

9

# CAT IN THE TREE

"Growing up on a homestead I had some interesting and exciting experiences. Probably my greatest adventure was the time Pa and I tangled with a mountain lion," John Wimple recalled.

"I was twelve years old. We were grouse hunting on the ridge behind the house. A grouse began drumming and Pa and I cautiously made our way toward the source of the sound.

"Pa suddenly remarked, 'John, look there!' His arm went up until he was pointing directly overhead, into a big leaf maple tree. Maybe forty feet above us was a tawny-colored mountain lion. It was stretched out on a limb and its long tail twitched back and forth.

"Pa reasoned, 'It wouldn't be safe having a mountain lion living this close to our homestead. Besides, he'd make a real nice rug. I'm gonna shoot him.'

"I stood back and watched Pa sight up into the tree. He pulled the trigger and was momentarily engulfed in a cloud of white smoke. I caught sight of the cat falling. When the smoke cleared a little I saw the cat had Pa pinned on the ground and there were all sorts of terrible noises; the gnashing of teeth, snarls, groans, moans and sharp cries.

"Pa managed to toss the rifle to me. I caught it and rather than watching what was going on I concentrated on reloading as quickly as possible. Once I had accomplished this task I thrust the muzzle of the rifle at the mountain lion and jerked the trigger.

"Pa had been mauled on his face and neck. He carried those scars with him to his grave."

# STAGECOACH RACE

"There has never been a stagecoach race like the one held at the 1911 Pendleton Round-Up," said the old-time cowboy. "There were two drivers going head to head — Spain, a tough, young buckaroo, and a seventy-year-old veteran name of Hutchison.

"The race covered two laps around the arena. Spain and Hutchison approached the starting line driving four-horse teams hitched to authentic coaches. How their high-spirited horses did prance! Why even a greenhorn could see they were anxious to run.

"The signal was given. They were off, racing for the first corner. Spain had the inside track and coming out of the corner he was leading. But Hutchison's horses were faster on the straightaway and as they approached the second corner the two hard-charging stagecoaches were, once again, dead even.

"The crowd suddenly gasped because it was plain to see that Spain had lost one of his lines. He did not have full control of his horses and yet he was standing, whipping his horses while the loose line flapped like a towel in a stiff breeze.

"Cowboy Zibe Morse recognized the potential for disaster. He sprung onto his horse, dug in with his spurs, rode hard and fast, leaned low at the edge of the boiling dust and somehow managed to grab the loose line and flip it to Spain.

"It appeared as if the race would surely end in a tie but coming down the last straightaway one of Hutchison's horses went down and this caused a chain reaction and a terrible wreck. Spain was the undisputed winner of the 1911 World Championship Stagecoach Race, the wildest stagecoach race I ever did see."

# TELL ME ABOUT FREIGHTING

"So you're studying about old-time transportation in school and want me to tell you about wagon freighting. That is a subject I do know a little something about," Grandpa said, tousling his grandson's hair.

"I drove freight wagon for nine years, until a company with trucks took over the route. I ran a six-horse team, pulling two wagons hooked in tandem. The first pair of horses was the lead team. They were the most intelligent and had to be alert and respond quickly to voice commands. Next was the swing team. They were matched for size and disposition. The wheelers, the team closest to the wagon, were my biggest horses and responsible for turning the wagon. When I needed a little extra pulling power on a long grade I called on the wheelers.

"A freighter was required to read the road, especially in the rainy season. If a puddle was fairly clear it meant the footing was generally solid but if it was oozing mud it was a bottomless pit. You avoided those places because if a teamster had to have another outfit pull him out, it meant you had to set up the driver at the next watering hole. That is, buy him a drink.

"Each freight outfit was known by its bells. They were fixed to the hames and sometimes the harness of the horses. Miles away you could tell who was coming by the sound of the bells. It was important others could hear because on the open roads there were blind corners and narrow spots. If you heard an outfit you pulled off at a turn out and waited.

"Freighters followed common courtesy on the road. Any driver not playing by the rules was asking for a scab on his nose. In this day and age the drivers of automobiles could take a lesson or two from us old-time freighters, they sure could."

# SHEEPHERDER'S STORY

"I had a little mishap back in 1914 that very nearly cost me my life," told Walter Catron.

"At that time I was herding sheep in Joseph Canyon. It was a fine spring morning and I was breaking camp while keeping an eye on the sheep scattered out grazing along the open face of a ridge. I put out my campfire, finished loading my pack horse, and went to tuck my rifle in the scabbard. I don't rightly know what happened except maybe my horse moved and somehow the trigger got hung up on something.

"The long and short of it was my rifle discharged and I got shot in the right leg. The slug hit high, near my front pocket, and traveled straight down my leg. Immediately I stripped off my shirt, tore it in half, applied a compress and managed to slow, but not stop, the bleeding. Unless I got to a doctor, and the nearest one was ten miles away, I knew I was a dead man.

"Gritting my teeth against the pain I pulled myself up and into the saddle, got myself situated and told my horse, 'Let's go, boy. Get me out of here.'

"I might have made it but, after climbing out of the canyon, there was a gate. I had to dismount to open it and did not have the strength to pull myself back on my horse. I started crawling, pulling myself along with my hands and elbows.

"That's when old man McWillett, a local homesteader, happened down the road and found me. He helped get me to Doc Gilmore's place. All I could offer McWillett was, 'Thank you for saving my life. I owe you one.'"

# RATTLIN' JACK

He was an old man, but his voice was still strong as he growled, "My God-given name is Jack Dillon, but I'm known far and wide by Rattlin' Jack.

"Got that moniker hung on me during my days driving stagecoach. I drove for the Wells Fargo company. Back then highwaymen were having a field day robbing the stage lines of gold shipments. But I came up with a suggestion that helped put them out of business.

"After being held up a time or two I came to realize that once a highwayman got the drop on the guard riding shotgun with me, chances were good he was gonna pull off the holdup. I told the Wells Fargo company to put another guard inside with the passengers. That way we doubled our chances of saving the express box.

"The company liked my idea and on the very next run I had two men riding shotgun, one on the seat next to me and a second inside the coach. Sure enough, at a narrow spot on the road where I'd been waylaid in the past, I heard the command, 'Halt!' I pulled to a stop. 'Lay down your gun.' The guard riding shotgun complied.

The first highwayman kept his rifle pointed in our direction while the second man reached for the strongbox. The guard inside the coach let him have a slug in the stomach and then he kicked open the door and gunned down the other bandit.

"It was over just that fast. Word quickly spread among the highwaymen that armed guards were riding with the passengers but it took another holdup or two to finally convince the desperadoes that their outlaw days were over and done with."

# REWARD

"Without a doubt the best work horses I ever did own were a matched set, white as driven snow; one a gelding, the other a mare," claimed homesteader Bill Rogers.

"I would step out of the house of the morning and the two of them always greeted me with a friendly nicker. They were intelligent, had fine dispositions and strong hearts. When I asked them to pull, they got right down and pulled. Why, if I'd of asked them to pull the earth out of orbit they would have tried.

"One spring morning I stepped out the back door and there was no nicker from my team. I crossed the barnyard and discovered my beautiful horses were missing. They had been stolen.

"I rode to all the neighbors asking if they'd seen my team pass that way. None had. I had posters printed and plastered them to fence posts and barns up and down the valley. I made note of an identifying mark, a wire cut scar on the left hind leg of the gelding. And I offered a reward, $500, which was a lot of money back in 1874.

"The posters did the trick. Two men brought a pair of brown work horses to a blacksmith on the Santiam Wagon Road. They said the gelding had thrown a shoe and wanted it replaced. During the process of forging a new shoe the smithy, who had seen the poster, detected the distinct odor of fresh dye and discovered the natural color of both horses was white, not brown. He checked for the telltale scar and alerted the sheriff. The thieves went to jail and to my great relief my team was returned to me. Once the dye washed away they were as good as new."

# PARTING OF THE WAYS

"Green McDonald and I were best of friends," stated Angus McPherson. "Were just like brothers.

"We came out west together and in all the years we knew each other there was only one subject we could not agree upon; in fact, we could not even discuss it. That was the issue of slavery. Green was from the deep South and believed slavery a divine institution. I, on the other hand, embraced the abolition of slavery.

"One Sunday Green came over for dinner. In a very solemn tone he informed me, 'Fort Sumpter has been fired upon. The South will no longer submit to interference by the North. This is war. And you, Angus, I suppose you will hold with the North?'

"I nodded in the affirmative.

"'I am siding with the Confederates. If the war comes to the West we shall be on opposite sides. But, Angus, if I have to face you, I do not believe I could kill you. I could never stain my hands with your blood. I will fire over your head.'

"He extended his hand and said, his voice tight with emotion, 'Then, old friend, we have come to a parting of the ways. Goodby.' We shook hands and Green turned away. My wife called out to him, imploring him, 'But Green, you and Angus have been such true friends for so long. Please, at least have a last meal together.'

"But he declined and in the intervening years we occasionally saw each other but we never exchanged any sign of recognition, nor spoke. I regret our friendship had to die over such a matter as slavery."

# BAD EGG

"The summer of 1900 a young man approached me on the street and called me by name. He introduced himself as Bill Johnson," recalled Grandpa.

"I thought I was a pretty good judge of character and I quickly sized up this young man. He was tall and skinny, had a weather-beaten face and a crippled right arm.

"'I'm fresh out of luck and my prospects for a change look mighty slim,' he told me. 'I was told you were an officer with the IOOF and I was wondering if you could help me since I am a member of the Nova Scotia lodge. I'm trying to get home. My father has come down mighty sick. I just picked up a letter from my mother at the post office....' He tapped an envelope in his breast pocket. 'She needs me home, needs me mighty bad.'

"I offered him twenty bucks but told him he would have to sign for it. He was agreeable. When I handed him a pen to sign the credit slip he claimed he did not know how to read or write and simply scratched a lopsided X.

"After two months and not a word from the borrower I wrote to the Nova Scotia IOOF lodge asking them to provide me with Johnson's address. I received a telegram in reply. This is what it said: That scoundrel has never been a member of this lodge STOP We have received hundreds of letters asking us to repay his loan STOP If this man calls on another lodge be advised to advance him a small sum and arrest him for obtaining money under false pretense STOP.

"I checked with other lodges and in short order ascertained that the young man had been making the rounds, using the crippled arm for sympathy and a myriad of pitiful stories to milk gullible lodge officials out of thousands of dollars. Plain and simple, the young man was nothing more than a bad egg."

# FLATHEAD

"I first came to the west coast to trap beaver," claimed the old man. "In those days it was the custom of some native people to flatten the heads of their children.

"It appeared to be a painless process and began shortly after birth when the bones in the infant's head were soft and malleable. The mother would fasten her papoose in a wooden cradle and place it so the baby looked skyward. A small box made of wood, perhaps four inches wide and nine inches long, filled with feathers and down would be carefully placed, longitudinally, upon the infant's forehead. The box would then be bound in place by wrapping leather strips about it. It was actually the weight of the feathers and the box that caused the malformation of the bones and not the tightness of the wrapping.

"The territory of the Flatheads ran from Puget Sound south to below the Columbia River and east as far as the Cascade Mountains. While in this region the natives did not fear capture and enslavement from others of their kind. But most tribes kept slaves. Slaves were never allowed to flatten their children's heads. Thus slaves were conspicuous creatures who rarely escaped once in the land of the Flatheads.

"Some of the early settlers said that because of their oddly shaped heads the natives were not as intelligent as the interior tribes. Actually they were among the most intelligent and progressive. They constructed permanent settlements, caught fish with seine and employed the use of many tools to make their work easier.

"The missionaries came and taught the natives the white man's God had created the human in his likeness and that it was a grave sin to reshape His work. Gradually, over a few decades the practice of flattening heads was discontinued.

"Where once a flat head was a sign of beauty, it became only the very old who had that distinction. And they were forced to live out their days in disgrace."

# SPEED TRAP

"As far as I know I was the first driver to ever be caught in a speed trap. That was back in April of 1908," recalled W.B. Stevens of Portland, Oregon.

"At the trial before the municipal judge the two patrolmen, Wellbrook and Cory, testified how they established their speed trap. They located a flat spot on Willamette Boulevard and used a stump near the road to measure off 440 yards. At this point they put down a stake. One man hid behind the stump and gave a signal with his arm when a car passed him; the other patrolman stood at the stake with a watch.

"The officers claimed that before I came along they timed four other automobiles that were going so fast and raising so much dust they could not make out the hand-lettered licenses on the rear of the speeding machines. According to Wellbrook and Cory, they clocked me at 30 miles per hour. What infuriated me was their claim I was a menace to every farm vehicle and pedestrian on the road.

"In my defense I called an elderly lady, one of the five passengers I had in my automobile at the time of the alleged infraction, and under oath she stated, 'I have very weak nerves and cannot stand high rates of speed. I am positive that we were bowling along at a speed no faster than a horse would trot.'

"Before the judge rendered his decision he said that, in his opinion, the officers could not have made a mistake, that it was a matter of timing and long division. He found against me but concluded, 'I am inclined to believe the offense was not a serious infraction. A five dollar fine will be sufficient.'"

# TOUGH MAN

"Toughest man I ever laid eyes on was S.E. Hankins. Don't rightly know what S.E. stands for. Never had the guts to inquire," Grandpa said.

"I well remember S.E. He was a big man, stood six feet three in his stocking feet and weighed well over two hundred pounds. He was healthy as a horse. And then, out of the clear blue, S.E. suffered severe stomach pains. He rode forty miles to the settlement to have Doc Ashford take a look and tell him what was wrong.

"Doc Ashford immediately diagnosed a ruptured appendix and said that unless the appendix came out, and in a hurry, S.E. was a dead man.

"'So what ya waitin' fer?' S.E. wanted to know. 'Cut me open.'

"Back in those days, the late 1800s, there were no hospitals in the vicinity. In fact, Doc Ashford did not have an operating table at his disposal. He improvised, removing a door from its hinges and placing it across two sawhorses.

"The operation took place under a kerosene lamp. The only anesthesia available was whiskey. S.E. took a couple of swallows, gritted his teeth and toughed out the pain. After the incision was closed Doc Ashford gave S.E. no better than fifty-fifty odds of pulling through.

"But ten days later S.E. remounted his horse and rode the forty miles home. Ten days after that he returned to breaking wild mustangs. He never bothered to have Doc Ashford remove his stitches. Nope. He plucked them out with his pocketknife.

"As far as I know, S.E. was the first man in these parts to have his appendix burst and removed, and live through the ordeal. But like I said, S.E. was tough as nails."

# DANCE IN BUFFALO SKULL

"This is a story of the little people who come alive after sundown," spoke a tribal elder.

"One black night, at the far edge of the plains, two balls of fire appear like glowing embers. Together, side by side, they move, flitting above the prairie grass. They grow larger, become the eyes of a terrible monster. In the darkness the body of the monster remains hidden. But it is there. You know it is, and the burning eyes come nearer, and nearer, and nearer.

"At the very heart of the level land there is a huge, old buffalo skull. Inside that skull the little people, assuming the form of field mice, are having a gay feast. They dance around a bonfire, hopping on their hind legs and holding up their tails, circling the fire as wee drums keep a strong, steady beat.

"Nearby a pack of wolves sits watching the glow as yellow light leaks from all the curious holes in the buffalo skull. In unison they point their noses to the sky and howl mournfully. But even this warning goes unheeded by the gay field mice. They continue to feast, nibbling on dried roots and venison. They sing and dance.

"All the while the fierce eyes silently creep toward the buffalo skull. A skinny finger of light reaches out to touch the skull and flicker at one of the eye sockets. A frightened mouse squeaks, 'Spirit of Buffalo!' and jumps out a hole in the back of the skull. The other mice, screeching and squealing, scramble from holes both large and snug and escape into the dark.

"And that my young people is our tribal legend of Dance in Buffalo Skull."

# MOVING WEST

"Times were tough in Nebraska. It finally came to the point where we could no longer make a living on the farm. We decided to pull up stakes, come west," LaVerne Easterday drawled.

"I rented a boxcar and used my team of Percherons to haul everything we owned to the train station. I loaded our wagon, farm machinery, household furniture, and even the dogs, turkeys, chickens, six head of milk cows, and the team in the boxcar.

"The railroad workers hooked our boxcar directly behind the locomotive. I protested, believing the whistle might spook the stock, but it was explained to me that if the boxcar was put farther back, there would be slack between the couplings and when the train moved forward or slowed the animals would likely be jerked off their feet.

"I stayed in the boxcar, fixing myself a bed in the wagon box. By the second day all was back to normal. The cows gave their customary number of gallons of milk and the chickens were back to laying an egg a day. I passed time peering through the slats in the boxcar and watching the country pass. At night I caught flashes of light from towns as we passed through, wondering to myself where in the world we might be.

"At one point, maybe in Utah, one of the milk cows began pawing the floor. I took a look and she was calving. The bull calf was born healthy and was up and sucking right away.

"We settled on a ranch in Idaho. The calf born in the boxcar grew strong and healthy. The following year we butchered it. The team of Percherons worked until one died at the age of twenty-three. I turned the other out to pasture. We still have the wagon but, of course, we don't use it any more."

# PAPER MONEY

"Gold lured me from my native state of Pennsylvania, first to California and then I drifted north to The Dalles, Oregon, which at the time was the gateway to the newly-discovered gold fields in the upper John Day country," Henry Wheeler said.

"I saw the need for a stage line that would run to the mines and in May 1864 I purchased horses and a stagecoach and made my first trip, carrying eleven passengers who paid forty bucks apiece for the privilege. After that I established a regular schedule and was soon handling the Wells Fargo business and contracting to carry the U.S. mail. The only real trouble I ever had was with Indians. In the four years of my stage operation the Indians killed or made off with eighty-nine head of horses.

"The closest call I had personally was September 7, 1866. I was driving through Bridge Creek canyon, where large sheltering rocks make an ideal hiding spot. Indians ambushed us and one slug struck me in the face, passing through both cheeks and blasting away my upper gum and some teeth. H.C. Page, who was riding shotgun, kept the Indians at bay while I, despite my injury, unhitched the lead team. Page and I sprang onto their backs and to escape we rode more than a hundred miles to The Dalles.

"A posse was sent out. They located the coach and the express box with the lid ripped off. Scattered around in the brush the posse recovered $10,000. Apparently the Indians did not know the value of paper money."

# THE QUOTE

"I came west to seek my fortune in the gold fields. One night, sitting around a campfire, I listened to a miner tell a fantastic tale about the Blue Bucket Mine. He claimed to have been there once and found gold nuggets lying on the top of the ground for the taking. But he was never able to relocate the spot. I went in search of the fabled Blue Bucket Mine," E.S. McComas said.

"Like many others before and after me I failed to locate the gold deposit. For my troubles I managed to collect a wound from an Indian arrow. I decided to give up the prospector's life and moved to Northeastern Oregon where I started the first newspaper in that region, the *Mountain Sentinel*.

"The highlight of my journalistic career, and the single event for which I will be most remembered, occurred in 1877 when I accompanied the peace commissioners to the Wallowa Valley. They were attempting to reach a settlement with Chief Joseph and thereby avoid any conflict with the Nez Perce Indians.

"Upon our arrival in the valley we found the area filled with Indians. Along with one of the scouts I rode to the main Indian camp, boldly approached Chief Joseph's tepee and requested a meeting.

"Chief Joseph was very sullen. His answers to my questions were short and to the point. Finally, I asked if he would be willing to leave this valley and live on a reservation. His answer proved to be the turning point that would, the following year, lead to the Nez Perce War. It is a quote that will live forever.

"I printed what this noble man said, word for word, in my newspaper: 'This has been home of my fathers as long as the oldest Nez Perce can remember. You can take all outside of this valley, but this valley is my home and I am going to fight for it and my children will fight for it. I have no more to say.'"

# ONE AT A TIME

"The Golden Rule was the working man's watering hole. Most any time, day or night, there would be buckaroos, railroaders, homesteaders and maybe a few dance hall girls lined up along the bar. It was the place to be if you were in Pendleton, Oregon. Beer was served by the glass as well as by the bucket," recalled one of the retired bartenders.

"The manager required that the bartenders keep track of each customer and how many beers they consumed. On New Years Eve, at the close of 1897, the Golden Rule threw a big celebration and at the stroke of midnight the manager of the Golden Rule hollered, 'All right, you yahoos, quiet down.'

"It took a few moments for the crowd to quiet and then the manager announced, 'On behalf of the Golden Rule I would like to present awards to some special customers. First of all, the Freeloader Award goes to Missouri John. During the past year he has managed to eat 1,107 of our free sandwiches. But to his credit he has consumed 2,136 glasses of beer.'

"The crowd cheered but the manager cut them short, 'Hold on now. Missouri John holds the sandwich record but he did not win the drinking contest.'

"'Who drank more than me?' challenged Missouri John.

"The manager ignored Missouri John, calling out, 'Mr. Douglas Glenn, will you please step forward.'

"Glenn presented himself and the manager gave him a $150 stickpin and shook his hand as he proclaimed, 'Mr. Glenn holds the one-year Golden Rule record. He has consumed 2,785 glasses of beer. That is an average of nearly eight beers a day, each and every day of the year. The first round of '98 is on me. Drink up, boys.'

"Douglas Glenn and Missouri John raised their glasses in a toast and counted — one."

# THE DEVIL AND THE SHEEP

"When I was a young man I herded sheep in the mountains and on the desert. I was forced to endure the harsh climate, the rugged terrain and the continual battle with the cattlemen who tried to drive all sheep from the range," Roy Leonard recounted.

"I composed a little poem which I do believe pretty well summarizes this bleak period of my life and puts things into proper perspective. The poem goes like this:

> Old Satan dreamed in his fiery bed,
> That he was kind and God was dead.
> That the high desert was a sunny State,
> In which to find himself a mate.
> So he swapped hell for the land of choice,
> And over his luck he began to rejoice.

"The next few stanzas tell how the devil was deceived into thinking lava rocks were lumps of black gold, that the bitter alkali water was wine, the arid sagebrush plains were covered with lush grass and how the falling snow was actually butterflies migrating through. The devil, he soon learns all this is not true. The rest of the poem goes:

> He gnashed his teeth, cursed and swore,
> He screamed until his throat was sore.
> 'It's just my luck!' he was heard to yell,
> 'I wish to God I was back in hell!'
> For three long days he thus did rage,
> Then went to town and caught the stage.
> 'Think what you please,' says he,
> 'But I hereby set all sheepherders free.
> For men in hell I will not keep,
> Who damn their souls by herding sheep.'"

# LONG GONE

"Funniest thing I ever saw," related Jim Weatherby, "happened years ago when I was running a mining camp trading post.

"We got in a shipment of double-action revolvers, the first in the country, and there was a steady parade of men who came in and wanted me to demonstrate the weapon. Late that afternoon an Indian wandered in and requested a demonstration. I explained the action, said it was not necessary to cock the hammer, that to fire, and fire repeatedly, all one had to do was squeeze the trigger.

"A miner, who evidently had been imbibing a great deal, happened in and in a loud, belligerent voice let it be known Indians were not welcome in camp. The Indian went to set down the loaded revolver, but he must have touched the trigger because all of a sudden there was a deafening roar and the quick 'zing' of a ricocheting bullet.

"The revolver hit the floor, discharged again and this time the slug buried itself in the wall a few scant inches from the miner's head. He made a lunge for the door. The Indian lunged, too. They collided. It was the miner who pushed his way out. He went stumbling up the street yelling at the top of his lungs, 'Indians! They're on the warpath!'

"Well, men spilled out from the bar, weapons drawn, looking for Indians. But my Indian customer was gone, long gone."

# A YOUTHFUL MISTAKE

"This is an embarrassing story for an old man to tell on himself. But I'll tell it anyway," said Owen Thompson.

"I was a young fellow, maybe sixteen or seventeen years old. I liked to hang around with a group of boys who were older than me and I was usually the brunt of a lot of their teasing.

"This one time I got the bright idea that we should go out mustanging. In those days there were a lot of horses running wild on the desert and I figured we could catch some and make a few dollars for our efforts. I was excited at the prospect until one of the boys said to me, 'You know how Indians like horses. I just hope we don't get scalped.'

"I took the warning to heart and bought a six-shooter. When we rode out to go mustanging I had the six-shooter strapped to my hip like a hero in a two-bit western.

"The round-up went smooth as silk. We collected over a hundred head of mustangs. Of course, my friends let me know that the most dangerous time, when Indians were most likely to attack, was on the drive home.

"At the first camp I told the others, 'Better put out a night guard.' I volunteered to ride the first shift.

"The sun was down and dusk was gathering as I made my rounds. There was enough light to see and I spotted movement on a hillside. Someone was leading away two horses. I hollered at the top of my lungs, 'Indians!' and drew my six-shooter.

"I waited for the others and warned them there was probably an entire war party of Indians just over the hill. We gave chase and in less than a mile we overtook an old Indian woman leading two Indian pack animals. It was an innocent mistake but the others teased me unmercifully about jumping to the wrong conclusion."

# THE TRAP

"I killed a nice buck and hung it from a tree limb outside the back door of my cabin. The next morning, when I stepped outside to carve off a steak for breakfast, the deer was missing," related Jack Murray.

"A man with a stomach for steak can get mighty perturbed at such a turn of events. I checked around and found evidence that a big cougar had stolen my venison. I fetched my rifle and set off after that thieving cat. The trail where the deer had been dragged was easy to follow. Maybe a quarter of a mile from the cabin, at the base of a rock outcropping, I located what was left of my deer. I had the feeling Mr. Cougar was nearby but I could not seem to spot him.

"Soon I had formulated a plan on how I was going to even the score. There was a forked tree growing nearby and I positioned my rifle in the crotch of that tree, wedged it down tight and made sure it pointed directly at the carcass. I stretched a length of rope between the carcass and the trigger of my rifle and then I went back to my cabin.

"That evening I was awakened by the hair-raising scream of a cougar. I lay there in bed with the covers pulled up to my chin and I imagined Mr. Cougar out there moving silently through the pine forest, moonlight streaming down. I must have fallen asleep because I came awake to the boom of a gunshot. Echoes bounced around between the hills. I just grinned, knowing my trap had been sprung. And the next morning, when I checked, I found a 200-pound cougar shot square between the eyes."

# FRIENDS

"I was only twelve years old when I took my first summer job, working in the grain harvest. I drove a team and wagon between the fields and the warehouse in town," related Mr. Umphlette.

"There was another driver, an older fellow name of Billy Barlow. He was all of thirty. I idolized him. He had sailed the seas, lived as a gentleman in San Francisco, buckarooed in Nevada and mined in Colorado. It seemed he had been everywhere and done everything.

"One day after unloading at the dock, Billy said me, 'I'm in need of a good timepiece. Let's swing by the jewelry shop for a look-see.'

"Billy had the jeweler lay out his entire selection of pocket watches and tell him the merits of each piece. Finally Billy stated, 'I've made up my mind. Tomorrow I'll draw my pay and be back.'

"Billy and I departed. Two miles from town we were overtaken by the jeweler and the constable. The jeweler pointed an accusing finger and snapped, 'One of you stole my watch and a gold chain.'

"The constable forced us to empty our pockets. He and the jeweler explored every nook and cranny in the wagons. But they found nothing and departed. As soon as they were out of sight Billy laughed. He stepped to my team and retrieved the watch and gold chain from where he had hidden them, tied to the underside of one my horse's mane.

"Right then and there I vowed that next time I would chose my friends more carefully."

# LASTING MEMORIAL

"When I was about your age, my dad used to take me grouse hunting," Jim Baker told his grandson. "One time I happened on an old shack. It looked deserted and, like young people will do, I decided to have a look inside.

"I pushed open the door. A Stetson hat hung from a set of deer horns. There were magazines on a low table. I blew off the dust, checked and found they were more than 20 years out of date. In the kitchen the table was set but the chairs were pushed back as if someone had gotten up quickly. At that point a queer sensation ran the length of my spine and made me shiver. I had the distinct feeling I was being watched.

"I was surprised by my father's voice calling to me. He stepped inside and I said, 'Looks like whoever lived here pulled out in a hurry.'

"'They did,' he said. 'The story is kind of a sad one. A man, his wife and their two children lived here. One morning, just as they were sitting down to breakfast, the telephone rang. It was an emergency call from a relative, someone sick or someone dying.

"'They skipped breakfast, got in their automobile and tore off down the road. Nobody knows what happened for sure, maybe a deer jumped out or the driver was blinded by the sun or there could have been a mechanical failure. Whatever it was caused them to wreck, running head on into a truck. They all died instantly.'

"I can't begin to explain, standing there in that deserted house, the heavy-hearted feeling that swept over me. But I can tell you, all my life I've remembered that and tried to make sure I drove safely."

# BLOODLESS CONFRONTATION

"I came to the Snake River country to winter range my cattle, but upon reaching Imnaha Canyon I was met by a band of disgruntled Indians and told to leave," recalled William Masterson.

"I told them I had as much right to the open range as the next man. They called for a council to be held the following day, and motioned to a rock slide in the distance, instructing me to round up all the other white men who were grazing stock in the area.

"Upon arriving at the council the Indians informed us we were trespassing. I spoke, said it did not matter what they liked, that we were staying. My words were translated by an old Indian woman wearing a blue soldier's overcoat. As she spoke some of the Indians began to drift away and work around behind us.

"This maneuvering greatly alarmed me and I whispered to the men who had come with me to make a break for the rock slide. We turned and ran, reached safety and waited there with our rifles resting over the tops of the boulders. I decided to try diplomacy one last time, calling out, 'There's plenty of room for all of us. Why don't we split the country; you take half and we take half.'

"And that was what we did. The Indians kept everything above the rock slide and we took everything below. Not a drop of blood was spilled.

"The following year the Nez Perce Indians went on the warpath. They were driven away from the Snake River country and the white man took all the land."

# INDIAN WAYS

Three old men were gathered around a potbelly stove, drinking black coffee and smoking hand-rolled cigarettes. One of them said, "I don't know what it is about the white man but he can't seem to leave the Indian well enough alone. He digs up burial grounds and sifts cremation sites looking for artifacts. And what does he do with them? He puts them on display in glass cases."

The second man said, "I know a special spot where the Paiute Indians stacked deer horns for hundreds of years. When the homesteaders came in they carted off wagonloads of antlers; made hat racks, archways and garden decorations out of them."

"We had a similar thing over on the coast," offered the third man. "We had what we called the Arrow Tree. It was a magnificent redwood stump. There were so many Indian arrows imbedded in it that it gave the appearance of quills sticking out of a porcupine.

"One time I was hiking the trail and happened to take a breather near the Arrow Tree. An Indian brave came along the trail. He never did see me. He walked up to the tree, offered a prayer to the Great Spirit and, looking through his quiver, he selected his best arrow, the one with the straightest shaft and most well-crafted point. He sent that arrow up and into the thick bark of the sacred tree and went on his way.

"You know what happened to that Arrow Tree? A white man chopped it down and cut it up into firewood."

# THE PRICE OF FAME

"My claim to fame occurred when I was twelve years old," Ed Hall related. "It was the summer of 1889 and a daredevil came to town with a balloon show. The advertisement promised that Professor P.H. Redmond would ascend in a balloon and parachute from the gondola to the ground.

"I attended the launch and watched as the professor called for the tether ropes to be dropped. The crowd surged forward and I found myself pushed to the front. One of the ropes snaked out, wrapped itself around my neck and I was jerked off my feet. Up, up, up we went and it was a terrible feeling hanging there so high above the ground. I grabbed the rope with my hands to keep from being strangled.

"The crowd below was screaming for the professor to bring the balloon down but he paid no attention until he happened to glance down. When he saw me he gave a startled gasp and turned the balloon back toward earth.

"I am quite sure the professor meant to land softly but in the excitement of the moment he misjudged, came down too fast and bashed me into the ground.

"As one might well expect, I was shaken and dazed from my ordeal. But by the time the crowd got to us, a distance of a couple miles, I was on my feet and moving under my own power.

"My fame was further enhanced when a photographer came forward. He had taken my picture as I dangled in space. Father bought the negative, had copies made and sold them for ten cents each. He made a small fortune."

# SHEEP SHOOTING

"I was a sheepman back in the day when the cattlemen were fighting for supremacy of the open range and making it a risky business to be a sheepman," E.F. Day said.

"One day in the summer of 1902 I received a telephone call from my camp tender. I reprimanded him, saying he was supposed to be out in the hills supplying the herders, not in town calling me on the telephone.

"He was in a panic and said he had been on Greenhorn Mountain, having breakfast with one of my herders, when a dozen men, faces smeared with lamp black, rode in. They demanded all sheep be removed from the range and to make their point they killed 30 head.

"I had a band of 2,400 head of yearling ewes on Greenhorn Mountain and lost no time riding there. No sooner did I arrive than the herder was yelling that the gang of sheepshooters had returned. A volley of rifle shots sent me diving for cover. I was forced to watch as sheep were slaughtered. It was a horrible thing to witness.

"When I could take no more of the bloodshed I called out, 'Stop! Stop! I'll move my sheep.'

"More than 300 sheep were killed outright or wounded so badly they could not travel. I had to leave them rather than risk the entire band. I promptly drove them from the mountains and sent a man up to make sure the wounded sheep were put out of their misery.

"From that day forward the cattlemen controlled that part of the open range. I never went back to Greenhorn Mountain."

# GRANDPA'S ALARM CLOCK

"The story I am going to relate happened in the fall of the year, nineteen and nine," E.D. Levy recalled.

"That particular night was quite chilly and when Grandma and I retired we lay in bed, the quilt pulled to our chins, and watched the moon and the way it reflected off the snow and bathed our room in stark, white light. Eventually we drifted off to sleep.

"Suddenly Grandma was shaking me awake. She whispered, 'There's a burglar outside. Do something!'

"I turned my head and sure enough, there was a shadow lurking at the window. I could see it was a man and that he had already managed to open the window and was beginning to thrust a foot inside our bedroom.

"The burglar was in the process of pulling his body through the opening and I was frozen with fear, knowing that my only weapon, a pistol, was locked in a trunk in the living room. It was at that instant I heard the *tick, tick, tick* of my alarm clock, a heavy old thing sitting on the night stand beside the bed. My right hand reached out and my fingers deftly wrapped around the cold metal case.

"I rolled and threw the alarm clock all in the same motion. It caught the burglar flush alongside the head. He let out a grunt and toppled backward through the window as the hammer of the alarm clock loudly rang the bell.

"I jumped out of bed and raced to the window. The burglar had gained his feet and was running away, holding both hands to his head. I closed the window and made sure it was locked. Then I retrieved my clock and turned off the alarm."

# BEAR IN THE TRAIL

"The summer of 1925 I was working for the Forest Service as a smoke chaser," related Cliff McGinnis. "A thunderstorm rolled through and one of the lookouts reported a fire about 12 miles from my station. I saddled up, slung the tools and rations on my pack mule and headed into the forest reserve.

"By the time I got to the fire it had burned itself out. I checked to make sure it was cold before I turned toward home. I traveled a couple miles, wasn't paying attention to much of anything, when a bear appeared in front of me. He was right there, smack-dab in the middle of the trail and he wasn't about to move.

"I tied the lead rope to a low branch, slid down off my horse and pulled my rifle loose from the scabbard. I squeezed off a shot and quick as a wink that bear was making beeline straight for me.

"I thought the best course of action was to get the heck out of there. I grabbed the horn and swung up onto the saddle. My horse spooked, swapped ends, got tangled up and all but pitched over. I don't rightly know how it happened but that hard-charging bear and I cracked heads. The collision knocked me silly, but I had presence of mind to grab a handful of mane and hold on while my horse ran away from the enraged bear.

"We flew past the mule and I hollered over my shoulder, 'It's every man for himself!' That mule broke loose and matched my saddle horse stride for stride. We raced plumb across the meadow before I pulled up.

"I called out to the bear, 'Sorry, Buster, didn't mean to upset you. What say you stay where you are and I'll take the long way and go out and around.'"

# THE THINKING MULE

"The best mule I ever had was Mac," boasted Roy Schaeffer, a high-mountain packer and trapper.

"I never had to worry my head about Mac. He moved at his own pace, picking his way along the trail, stopping at tight spots to make sure before trying to squeeze through. He stepped around obstacles rather than take a chance of bumping or scraping the pack.

"I'm sure Mac understood every word I said. In fact, all I had to do was think something and nine times out of ten he would catch on and do it. He was more human than he was mule.

"Mac always ate breakfast with me. He loved pancakes. But one morning, after getting his normal short stack, Mac began acting strangely. He refused to leave me alone and made a general pest of himself. He kept nudging me with his head. I asked him, 'What the heck is wrong with you?' He kept at it. Finally, when I had the string ready to go, Mac took off down the trail in the wrong direction. I whistled, called to him, but there was no turning him.

"I figured maybe that mule knew something I didn't, so I turned the string around and followed. Sure enough, in a couple hours it started dumping snowing and it kept snowing all that long day.

"At evening camp I built up a warm fire, cooked a batch of hotcakes and let Mac eat his fill. It was the least I could do because if we had been caught in the mountains, in that snow, we would have been trapped and might all have starved to death."

# PIRATES!

"Spent my life sailing the seven seas, but I've never seen the likes of what happened back in the summer of 1910," related the white-bearded sailor.

"I was with the crew of the *Buckman*. We had hauled food and supplies from San Francisco to Alaska and were scheduled to carry a shipment of gold on our return leg but the gold shipment did not arrive before our departure.

"We sailed south and off the mouth of the Umpqua River two passengers, a man and a boy, stormed the bridge with their weapons drawn. The man ordered the boy to stand guard and shoot any of us who moved while he went below deck to find the captain. A moment later there came the sharp report of two shots.

"At that point the boy, knowing he was now involved in murder, lost his guts. He ran away.

"The older man returned, marching several members of the crew in front of him. He marched us all to the wheelhouse where he ordered the first mate to steer for shore. As we neared the Umpqua bar we hit rough water and the gunman's attention was momentarily diverted. The crew seized this opportunity to make a break for it. We scattered, taking refuge behind lifeboats, water barrels and coils of rope.

"'Come out! Show yourselves!' he screamed and when we did not appear he began to roam the deck looking for targets. I made my way to my cabin, retrieved my pistol and when I had the chance I shot and killed the pirate.

"We found the boy hiding under his bunk, crying hysterically. He never stood trial for his part in the piracy and the killing of our captain. The rest of his days were spent confined in an insane asylum."

44

# COMPROMISING SITUATION

"For many years I worked as a clerk in Mr. Simpson's hardware store," stated M.W. Chandler. "One day he informed me he had been called out of town quite unexpectedly and, since he had many valuable things in his home, he asked if I would stay at his residence while he was away.

"The first night I spent at Mr. Simpson's home I found the sleeping accommodations to be quite comfortable. And as is my custom, I opened the bedroom window because I do enjoy the fresh air.

"I awoke to a bright, clear dawn, a day filled with promise. I began to dress and to my utmost bewilderment I discovered my trousers were not where I had placed them over the back of a chair. I searched high and low without success. Then I chanced to look out the window and judging from the evidence left behind it was evident that some person had set a washtub beneath the window. Seeing me sleeping in the bed, and realizing that if they attempted to enter the room they might very well be caught, this person had procured a long pole, pushed this through the open window and stole my trousers.

"I went to Mr. Simpson's closet and tried on a pair of his trousers, but he was so much shorter and thinner than I that there was no way his trousers would fit me. In the end I had to flag down a passerby and request his assistance.

"When I attempted to show this man my gratitude I realized the thief had taken not only my trousers but also my wallet. All I could offer was a heartfelt, 'Thank you, sir, for helping me out of a very compromising situation.'"

# PISTOL-PACKING PREACHER

The children in Sunday school always paid attention to the stories and lessons delivered by the Reverend Robert C. Lee.

Reverend Lee was born in England and instructed in the classical arts. He was a child piano virtuoso and could speak seven languages. At age nineteen he ran away from home to explore the world, joining the crew of a sailing ship bound for the coast of Zanzibar.

For two decades he sailed the high seas. Then one day he stepped ashore and announced he was turning his attention inland, that for the remainder of his life he would spread the word of the Lord.

In his later years one of Reverend Lee's favorite stories to tell the Sunday school children was about the time he ran the devil out of Huntington, a railroad town on the Oregon and Idaho border. He said, "When I arrived in town I looked up and down the main street, which was nothing more than a dreary collection of saloons and dance halls, and announced that I was going to clean up this cesspool of sin.

"In response I was threatened and shots were fired at my home. Come Sunday a large number of dance hall girls, sullen drunks and glinty-eyed gamblers came to my church to confront me. I faced the congregation, threw open my coat and withdrew a pair of revolvers. I laid a revolver on one side of the Bible and the other on the opposite side. In a loud voice I proclaimed, 'If there is any disturbance in my church, any disturbance whatsoever, I encourage each of you to remain seated. I do not want any innocent person to be inadvertently injured by a stray bullet.'

"On that Sunday a number of residents of Huntington turned to the Lord and away from their lives of crime. They became law-abiding citizens. And now, boys and girls, let us turn our attention to today's lesson. Please open your prayer books to page...."

# GOOD LUCK BAD LUCK

"I had a friend, Billy Martin, who was the fastest runner around our part of the country," related George Olds. "The summer of 1884 a group of well-heeled men from outside the area proposed a foot race between Billy and the supposed champion of the United States, a man named Kettleman. To stimulate the betting they offered Billy a twelve-yard head start in a hundred-yard dash.

"We all knew how fast Billy was and, as might be expected, a great deal of money was placed on the hometown boy. Billy went into training. His handler, a blacksmith, wagered his business and all his worldly possessions. I, too, placed a sizable bet on Billy.

"As I was traveling to the site of the race, I happened to notice a horseshoe lying along the side of the road. I took this as a sign of good luck and upon arriving in town I promptly doubled my bet.

"The runners took their marks, Billy twelve yards in front of Kettleman. Within a few strides it was evident Kettleman was far and away the more powerful runner. And yet I clung to the possibility Billy could hold his lead, but the distance between the runners quickly vanished. Kettleman crossed the finish line and continued to run another hundred yards. He leaped into a waiting hack and was driven away at a high rate of speed.

"It was later estimated that the local folks had been bilked out of more than $22,000 by the out-of-town syndicate. On the way home I stopped where I had spotted the lucky horseshoe and, much to my chagrin, discovered it was a mule shoe which of course, as everybody knows, brings nothing but bad luck."

# NINE-QUART COAT

"Sure I was a bootlegger," claimed Louis Johnson. "Everybody knew it, but nobody could prove it.

"About the closest call I had to getting caught was the time I almost sold a bottle to a revenuer. The instant he reached in his pocket I had an overpowering premonition he was going to pull out either a pistol or a badge. I grabbed back the bottle and ran.

"There were cops all over the place but I managed to dash into an alley. I ditched my coat and attempted to walk out of there like any ordinary stiff. Of course, the flatfoots grabbed me, arrested me and unceremoniously deposited me in the hoosegow.

"At my trial the federal prosecuting attorney entered my coat, the one I ditched in the alley, into evidence as Exhibit A. He made quite a big deal out of it and, in fact, he referred to it as the Nine-Quart Coat, demonstrating for all to see how nine quart bottles could be cleverly tucked into concealed pockets in the liner.

"He said, 'This coat is a vehicle, a contrivance if you will, for transporting illegal liquor. It falls under the same provision of the National Prohibition Act and should be confiscated just as rum-running cars and boats are.'

"My attorney, Allan Byron, pleaded for common sense. He claimed, 'If we allow the court to confiscate a man's coat, what next? His trousers? If every man with a hip flask is required to forfeit his trousers, I would bet two out of every three men will be striding around town in longjohns.'

"The judge ultimately decided the Nine-Quart Coat should go to jail. They could not prove it was my coat. I kept my mouth shut and never admitted nothin'. I walked out of the courtroom a free man, stepped around the corner to the men's shop and purchased a new coat."

# A FRIEND

"It is a good thing to treat your fellow man with friendship, but there are individuals who do not deserve your friendship," counseled James Hemenway.

"I met just such a man the winter of 1914. His name was Mullen and he was a drifter, a hobo, if you will. The first time I laid eyes on him he lunged at me from an alleyway demanding, 'Money for food!'

"I felt sorry for him. It was obvious he was down on his luck and I invited him home with me. I gave him dry clothes, fed him and provided him a dry, warm place to sleep. During the time he stayed with me his skinny frame took on weight and his spirits improved.

"The weather warmed and I suppose he was bitten by the wander bug because one day he informed me, 'I've got to be on my way. Someday I'll repay you. I swear I will.'

"Scarcely a month later I received a letter from Mullen. He was in Casper, Wyoming and had hastily scribbled, 'I've hit it big. Oil! Come and share in my good fortune.'

"There were several more encouraging letters from my friend, boasting of riches and the opulent lifestyle he was leading. At last I decided to join him. I took passage on the train, arrived in Casper and asked at the hotel where I might find Mr. Mullen, the man who had brought in the oil gusher.

"The clerk laughed in my face, said, 'The only oil Mr. Mullen is likely to be in would be tar and feathers.'

"I checked around and it became quickly apparent that Mullen, after a relatively short stay, had worn out his welcome in Casper. He had hopped an eastbound freight and was long gone. I bought a ticket for home and I do admit that my faith in mankind was sorely shaken."

# SNAKES

"There were always a lot of rattlesnakes around the home place," said John Crawford, who claimed a homestead on the north side of the Columbia Gorge.

"They nested up in the rocky cliffs and I was constantly having trouble with snake-bit dogs and cattle. And the family, we all had to be on the alert. We checked before we stepped off the porch, lifted boards away from us and looked under them. Rattlesnakes were everywhere. Once we even found a snake curled up in the wood box.

"Snakes hibernate during winter and emerge from their dens when the weather warms. One spring morning I packed my rifle up to the rattler den. I did not have to wait long before I saw a snake head poke from a six-inch hole in the rock bluff. I let the snake come all the way out before I shot.

"For the best part of an hour I kept my position, firing at snakes, and when I ran out of ammunition, I went to the opening and counted dead snakes. There were forty-five of them, one for each cartridge I had fired. And still more snakes slithered out from the opening. I departed a little bit disheartened, knowing I had done very little to reduce the population of snakes.

"To give you an idea of just how many snakes we had to content with — when they blasted the rock bluff to build the North Bank Railroad a great den of snakes was uncovered. It was cold, the snakes were drowsy and so the crew was able to dispatch them with clubs and rocks. They counted over a thousand dead snakes."

# CAPITOL FOR A DAY

"I was at Meacham, Oregon, the day the tiny town at the top of the Blue Mountains was named the capitol of the United States," Grandpa claimed.

"It was the third of July, 1923. The transcontinental highway was being dedicated, replacing the Old Oregon Trail, and the main attraction of the day was an appearance by President Warren G. Harding.

"The President came to Oregon on the train. He stepped down from his private car and was decked out in trousers, a plain straw hat, blue coat and a badge that read *President Harding*. The badge wasn't necessary. Everyone knew who he was.

"He took his place at the reviewing stand and the show got underway. Across the meadow a line of covered wagons came into view. Driving the teams of oxen, mules and horses, and walking alongside the wagons were old pioneers who had crossed the Oregon Trail in its heyday. The President saluted them. Behind the pioneers came a procession of Indians dressed in feather bonnets, scarlet blankets and their faces colored with paint. Following the Indians was a procession of automobiles.

"A long list of politicians and dignitaries spoke and then finally President Harding was introduced. He ended his eloquent speech by announcing that the old Oregon Trail was officially closed, and he welcomed a new era by opening the new transcontinental automobile highway. The crowd, estimated at 15,000 strong, cheered wildly.

"Today a rock monument marks the spot where President Harding once stood and proclaimed Meacham to be the official Capitol of the United States for a single day, way back in the summer of 1923."

# THE BANK

"I was a young county minister, traveling the back roads of the west," Reverend William Selleck related.

"One time, it was the summer of 1913, I found myself in a bustling settlement. It took most of my pocket money for a room at the hotel and when I asked the clerk to cash a check for me he stated it was the policy of the hotel not to cash personal checks.

"I looked out the window and between awnings saw the word BANK printed in large block letters. I went across the street, reached for the doorknob, opened it and stepped across the threshold. The door slammed shut behind me.

"The interior was like no bank I had ever set foot inside. While my eyes began to slowly adjust to the dim light my other senses fed a constant stream of information to my brain. There was a low din of voices and it sounded as if cards were being shuffled. I smelled smoke in the air and another unpleasant odor that I could not immediately identify.

"'Reverend, what are you doing in here?' a husky voice boomed.

"'I need to cash a check,' I answered meekly.

"Upon making this declaration I was greeted by a loud chorus of laughter. Suddenly I had no trouble identifying that vile smell. It was the devil's brew — beer.

"One of the men hollered, 'Reverend, you better step outside fer a look-see. This here's the Bank Saloon.'"

# GETTING AROUND

"Grandpa, I was just wondering, back in the old days how did you go places in the winter?" the boy wanted to know.

"We had bobsleds and cutters," his grandfather answered. "Bobsleds were normally fashioned from an old wagon box and double skids. They were used for chores around the farm. Some of my favorite memories are of frosty mornings in the pasture; setting the team so they would make a slow, wide circle while I pitched loose hay to the cows and calves.

"The bobsled was the workhorse of the farm but nobody used a cutter for chores. Cutters were purchased from an implement dealer and were strictly for pleasure. A cutter was a finely crafted sled, a thing of real beauty.

"A cutter was used for social visits, rides to the Saturday night dances and trips to town. The livery in town had several cutters that they rented to traveling salesmen and others who had occasional business in the country. They were fancy outfits, painted bright red, and pulled by matched teams with coal-black harness and sweet-sounding bells. Driving an outfit like that a young man could make quite a dashing appearance.

"When I was courting your grandmother I used to rent a cutter. We would pull a black bearskin rug over our laps and go for spirited rides. There could be a biting cold wind and blowing snow but we never took notice. We did have fun.

"In fact, we were riding in a cutter when I asked your Grandma to marry me. So you see, for me, a cutter has an extra special significance."

# BETTER DAYS

"I'm an old man now but they've been calling me Old Tom Petit as far back as I remember. In fact, on the day I was born my mommy called me Old Tom Petit.

"My claim to fame is that I was considered one of the best stagecoach drivers in the West. Ask anyone and they will tell you Old Tom Petit was the real deal.

"The happiest times of my life were spent on the high seat of a stage, hands full of lines, four-horse team out in front running at an easy lope. I drove stage across the deserts of Nevada, over the mountains of Oregon and Idaho, and was even down south in California. Drove a lot of miles and you might guess I saw more than my fair share of highwaymen.

"When you sign on to drive a stagecoach you give your word to the company that you will do your best to deliver your passengers and freight to their destination safe and sound. Besides highwaymen there were a lot of other dangers out on the road. I've seen nasty weather — blizzards with the temperature thirty below and the wind blowing the snow so you couldn't see your horses, floods that washed the road out from under me, and in the summer it could be 110 in the shade with no shade anywhere in sight.

"I guess all the miles and the extremes in weather must have settled in my bones. The doctors tell me I have rheumatism and arthritis. I'm all crippled up. Can't get around no more. All Old Tom Petit can do is sit in this rocking chair and tell stories of better days."

# OL' EPHRAIM

"Been a b'ar hunter all my life," Frank Clark claimed. "Know everything there is to know about b'ar.

"All those years tramping around in the woods the worst b'ar I came across was Ol' Ephraim. He was a big grizzly. To give you an idea of just how big he was; one time I saw where Ol' Eph bit clean through a six-inch aspen tree. It just so happened that where he took the bite was nine feet eleven inches off the ground. I had to stand on the back of my saddle horse to measure it.

"Ol' Eph had a distinctive track, three toes on one foot. As a cub he must have gotten his foot caught in a trap. That encounter made him a wary cuss. He always managed to stay one jump ahead of me and he would taunt me with a variety of tricks, like using a stick to spring my trap and steal my bait.

"One day I came across a fresh b'ar wallow and sure enough there was that three-toed track. I put out a set and traveled up the trail about a mile before I set camp.

"In the middle of the night I was awakened by a God-awful roar. I laid there in my bedroll, stars splashed 'cross the sky and the moon coming up over the ridge, listening to the sounds from down by the wallow — all the roaring, rampaging, bellowing, groaning, whining and whimpering. I never slept another wink that long night. Come first light I slipped down to the wallow. The woods were dead quiet until, all of a sudden, Ol' Eph raises up from behind a windfall and growls at me. I shoved the muzzle of my rifle into his gaping mouth and pulled the trigger.

"After that I was shaking so bad I had to sit down for a spell. You know, after chasing that b'ar for ten years, I felt a little remorseful the hunt was over."

# SEASONS

"Far away over the mountains lived a people who controlled winter and summer. They kept winter and summer in leather bags and released them only when it benefitted them," the old Indian told his grandson.

"One winter was very cold and long and our people ran low on food. They were starving. The most skillful warrior was sent to steal summer from the distant village.

"The night he arrived the leather bags were guarded by a woman. The warrior surprised her and before she could give the alarm he forced pine pitch in her mouth and stole the bag of summer.

"The woman ran through the village wildly waving her arms, but because of the pine pitch in her mouth she was not able to say anything. Soon it was discovered what had happened. The best runners were sent out to chase down the intruder.

"Within a few hours the runners were within sight of the warrior who had stolen the bag containing summer. They called for him to stop. But the warrior had a plan. He stopped suddenly and gave the bag a mighty toss. It flew very high into the sky, went up and over the mountains. When it came down our medicine man was there to catch it. He instantly transformed himself into a fierce grizzly bear and tore apart the laces, opened the bag and released summer.

"A Chinook wind made the canyon moan and the pine trees gave a long sigh. The snow began to melt. The camas began to bloom. The ducks and geese returned. The deer and elk came down from the mountains. Fish ran in the stream. Our tribe was saved.

"And that, my grandson, is the story of how the seasons of the year were created."

# CABIN FEVER

"Worst case of cabin fever I ever did suffer was in the winter of 1914," old man Bakke related. "At the time I was living up Whiskey Creek, nearest neighbor was 20 miles away but it might as well have been 200 miles, or 2,000 miles for that matter, because it snowed so much and was so bitterly cold all I could do was sit inside, feed wood into the stove and try to stay warm.

"One afternoon I heard a long, lonely howl. I thought I was hearing things but, still, I was so starved for any type of companionship that I jumped up, grabbed my accordion, raced to the door, threw it open and began to play, hoping to lure my visitor into view.

"My music cut through the thin, gray fog, skipped across the crust of the white snow and frolicked through the timbered hills. I played more beautifully than I ever played before or since, and presently a single coyote stepped into view, followed by a dozen or more. The entire pack stood there unmoving, heads cocked, ears perked, staring straight at me.

"Something in my mind must have snapped for all at once I was gripped by fear. What if these wild animals were looking at me as their meal? It had been a terrible winter and surely they were hungry. I stepped back, slammed the door, and leaned against it.

"The pack of coyotes chose that moment to lift their voices in song. I could not resist. I flung open the door and provided accompaniment to their feral refrains. As the music flowed tears ran unashamedly down my cheeks. And then, as suddenly as it had begun, the serenade ended. The coyotes silently slipped away into the timber. My heart was beating so wildly I had to lie down. It was an odd thing, but after that encounter, all that long winter, I never again felt lonely."

Rick Steber's Tales of the Wild West Series is available in hardbound and paperback books featuring illustrations by Don Gray. Current titles in the series include:

*OREGON TRAIL* Vol. 1
*PACIFIC COAST* Vol. 2
*INDIANS* Vol. 3
*COWBOYS* Vol. 4
*WOMEN OF THE WEST* Vol. 5
*CHILDREN'S STORIES* Vol. 6
*LOGGERS* Vol. 7
*MOUNTAIN MEN* Vol. 8
*MINERS* Vol. 9
*GRANDPA'S STORIES* Vol. 10
*PIONEERS* Vol. 11
*CAMPFIRE STORIES* Vol. 12
*TALL TALES* Vol. 13
*GUNFIGHTERS* Vol. 14
*GRANDMA'S STORIES* Vol. 15
*WESTERN HEROES* Vol. 16

**Other books written by Rick Steber —**

| | |
|---|---|
| *NO END IN SIGHT* | *HEARTWOOD* |
| *BUY THE CHIEF A CADILLAC* | *ROUNDUP* |
| *BUCKAROO HEART* | *LAST OF THE PIONEERS* |
| *NEW YORK TO NOME* | *TRACES* |
| *WILD HORSE RIDER* | *RENDEZVOUS* |

If unavailable at local retailers, write directly to the publisher for a free catalog.

**Bonanza Publishing**
Box 204
Prineville, Oregon 97754